EDITH NEWLIN CHASE   YOLAINE LEFEBVRE

Secret Dawn

FIREFLY BOOKS

The illustrations for this book were painted in watercolors. The artist drops her colors on soaking wet paper, letting them flow and blend freely. This technique is called "wet on wet." For reference, photographs were used, including some of the author's daughter and home.

The book was designed in Quark XPress, with type set in 24 point Giovanni Book.

A FIREFLY BOOK

Published in the U.S. in 1996 by:
Firefly Books (U.S.) Inc.
P.O. Box 1338
Ellicott Station
Buffalo, New York 14207

Cataloguing in Publication Data

Chase, Edith Newlin
  Secret dawn

A poem.
ISBN 1-55209-028-0

1. Children's poetry, American.   I. Lefebvre, Yolaine, 1950-   II. Title.

PZ8.3.C358Se 1996   j811'.54   C96-930445-5

Original text by Edith Newlin Chase, copyright © 1996. Original illustrations by Yolaine Lefebvre, copyright © 1996. Published by arrangement with North Winds Press.

6 5 4 3 2 1   Printed in Canada by DW Freisen   6 7 8 9/9

To my sister Martha
Who remembers still
Our fun in rolling pumpkins
Down our hill!
E.N.C.

To my children, Lyne and Dominic.
May they follow their inner road
towards the essential.
Y.L.

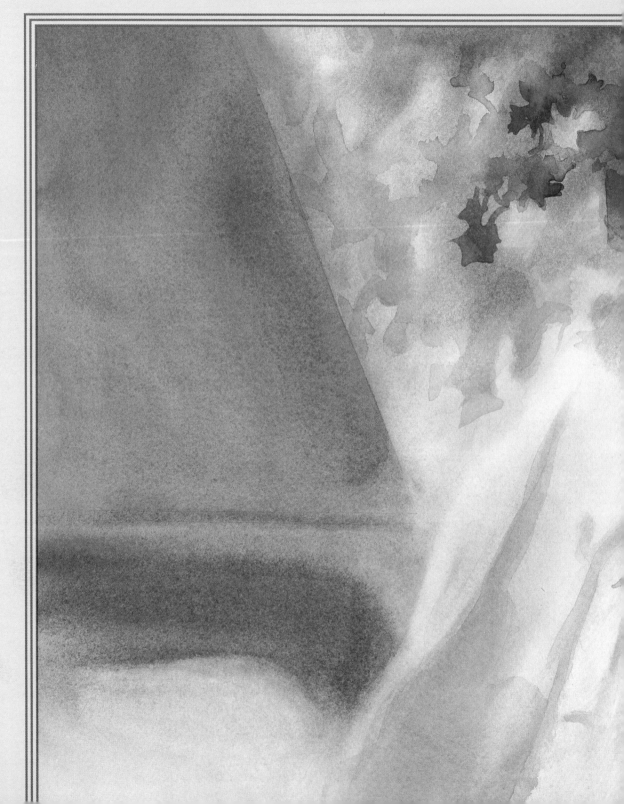

When the first thin light comes creeping
Up the early edge of day,

And the household still is sleeping,

Then I dress and slip away

To the place that I am keeping
For my secret hideaway.

Stealing toward the giant billow
  Of a tree across the lawn,

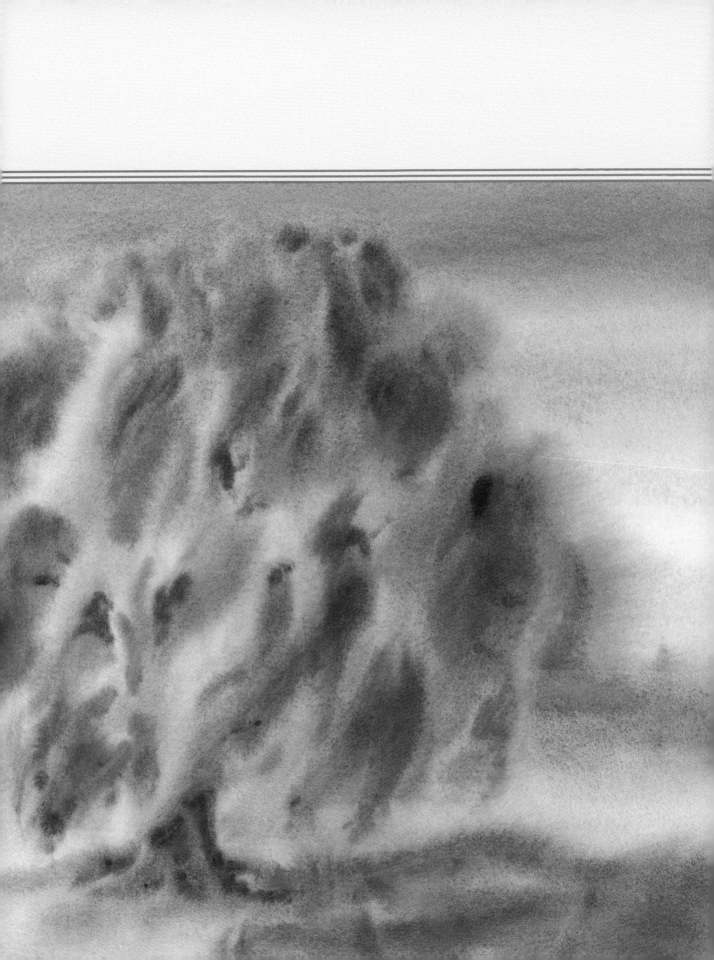

Like a leafy mammoth pillow
In the dim delight of dawn,

Up I climb into my willow
   While the night is hardly gone.

Up in the willow is wispy and whispery,
Silent and silvery, misty with mystery!

Nobody else in the world is awake!
Nobody knows how the little leaves quake.

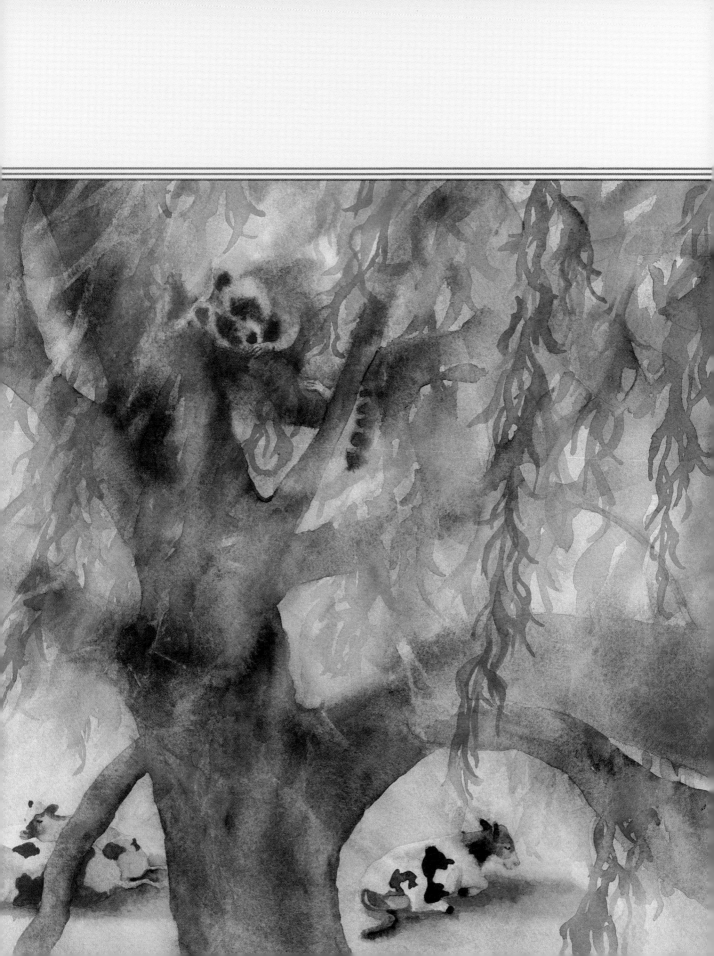

Nobody knows that the willow is mine.
Nobody knows of my shadowy shrine.

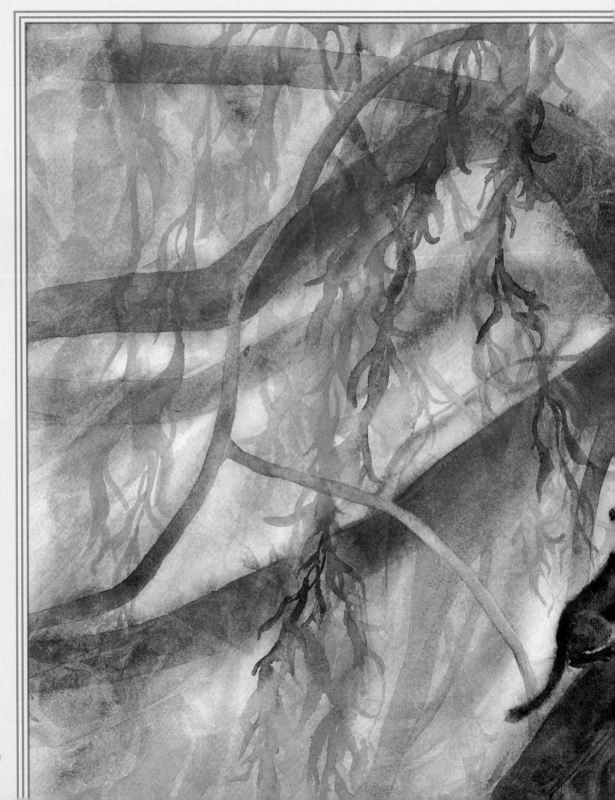

Nobody knows of the place where I hide
My mystery box with treasure inside.

Nobody knows of my notebook thin
Nor the stub of a pencil for writing in

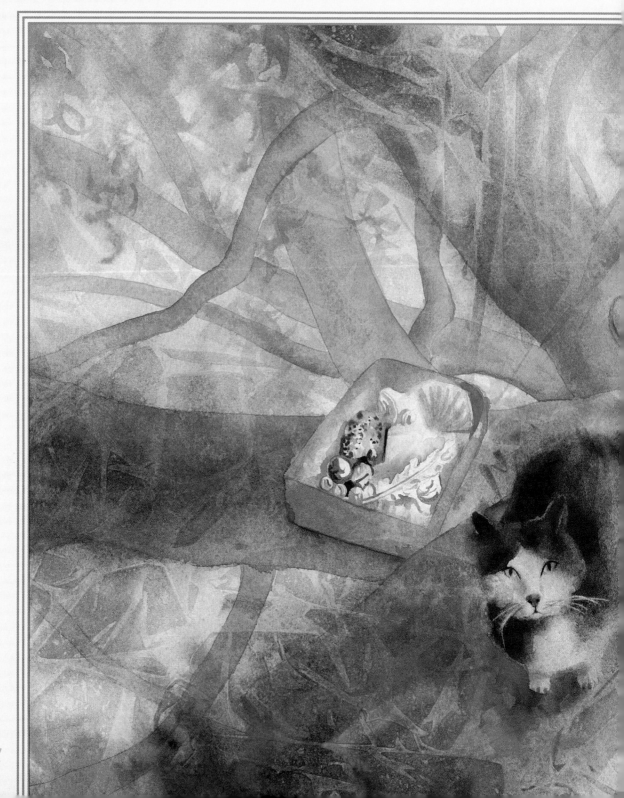

The secret thoughts and the secret rhymes
That I think to myself and write sometimes.

Nobody knows of my favourite tree
 Where we are alone—

My secret and me!